SILLY VERSE FOR KIDS AND ANIMALS

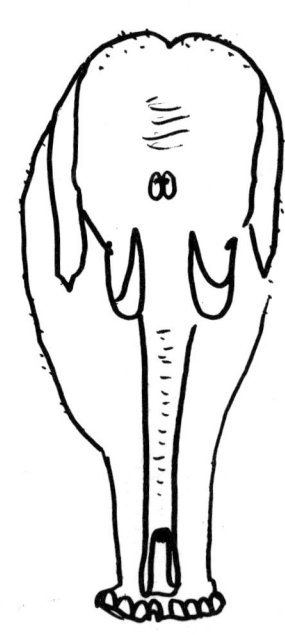

SPIKE MILLIGAN
SILLY VERSE FOR KIDS AND ANIMALS

M & J HOBBS
in association with
MICHAEL JOSEPH

This edition first published in Great Britain by
M & J Hobbs,
55 Wellington Close, Hepworth Way,
Walton-on-Thames, Surrey and
Michael Joseph Ltd,
44 Bedford Square, London WC1
1984

© 1984 Spike Milligan Productions Ltd.

All Rights Reserved. No part of this publication may be reproduced, stored in a retrieval system, or transmitted in any form or by any means, electronic, mechanical, photocopying or otherwise, without the prior permission of the Copyright owner.

British Library Cataloguing in Publication Data

Milligan, Spike
  Silly verse for kids and animals.
  I. Title
  821'.914   PR6063.I3777

ISBN 0 7181 2404 9

Printed in Great Britain by Hollen Street Press, Slough and bound by Hunter & Foulis, Edinburgh.

CONTENTS

Silly Verse for Kids . . .   7

String	9
Mary Pugh	11
Tell me little woodworm	13
Hipporhinostricow	15
I've never felt finer!	17
Said the General	19
Two children (small)	21
Granny	23
Hello Jolly Guardsman	25
To-day I saw a little worm	27
Teeth	29
Look at all those monkeys	30
Can a parrot	31
I'm not frightened of Pussy Cats	33
Down the stream the swans all glide	35
On the Ning Nang Nong	37
The Land of the Bumbley Boo	39
There was a young soldier called Edser	41
You must never bath in an Irish Stew	43
Hello Mr Python	45
A thousand hairy savages	47
The Bongaloo	49
My sister Laura	50
Failure	51
I once knew a Burmese horse	53
My daddy wears a big black hat	55
Maveric	56
On the Bright Azurian Sea	59

. . . and Animals   61

Part One: Animals	63
Part Two: Milliganimals	93
Part Three: The Bald Twit Lion	113

SILLY VERSE FOR KIDS...

FOREWORD

Most of these poems were written to amuse my children; some were written as the result of things they said in the home. No matter what you say, my kids think I'm brilliant.

S. M.

STRING

String
Is a very important thing.
Rope is thicker,
But string,
Is quicker.

P.S. The meaning of this is obscure
      That's why, the higher the fewer.

MARY PUGH

Mary Pugh
Was nearly two
When she went out of doors.
She went out standing up she did
But came back on all fours.
The moral of the story
Please meditate and pause:
Never send a baby out
With loosely waisted draws.

TELL ME LITTLE WOODWORM

Tell me little woodworm
Eating thru the wood.
Surely all that sawdust
Can't do you any good.

Heavens! Little woodworm
You've eaten all the chairs
So *that's* why poor old Grandad's
Sitting outside on the stairs.

HIPPORHINOSTRICOW

Such a beast is the Hipporhinostricow
How it got so mixed up we'll never know how;
It sleeps all day, and whistles all night,
And it wears yellow socks which are far too tight.

If you laugh at the Hipporhinostricow,
You're bound to get into an awful row;
The creature is protected you see
From silly people like you and me.

I'VE NEVER FELT FINER!

'I've never felt finer!'
Said the King of China,
Sitting down to dine—
Then fell down dead—he died he did!
It was only half past nine.

SAID THE GENERAL

Said the General of the Army,
'I think that war is barmy'
So he threw away his gun:
Now he's having much more fun.

TWO CHILDREN (SMALL)

Two children (small), one Four, one Five,
Once saw a bee go in a hive.
They'd never seen a bee before!
So waited there to see some more.
And sure enough along there came
A dozen bees (and all the same!)
Within the hive they buzzed about;
Then, one by one, they all flew *out*.
Said Four: 'Those bees *are* silly things,
But *how* I *wish* I *had* their *wings!*'

GRANNY

Through every nook and every cranny
The wind blew in on poor old Granny;
Around her knees, into each ear
(And up her nose as well, I fear).

All through the night the wind grew worse,
It nearly made the vicar curse.
The top had fallen off the steeple
Just missing him (and other people).

It blew on man; it blew on beast.
It blew on nun; it blew on priest.
It blew the wig off Auntie Fanny—
But most of all, it blew on Granny! !

HELLO JOLLY GUARDSMAN

'Hello Jolly Guardsman
In your scarlet coat:
It reaches from below your tum
To half way up your throat.'

'Tell me jolly Guardsman
When you're off parade
What kind of clothes do you put on?'
'Civvies I'm afraid.'

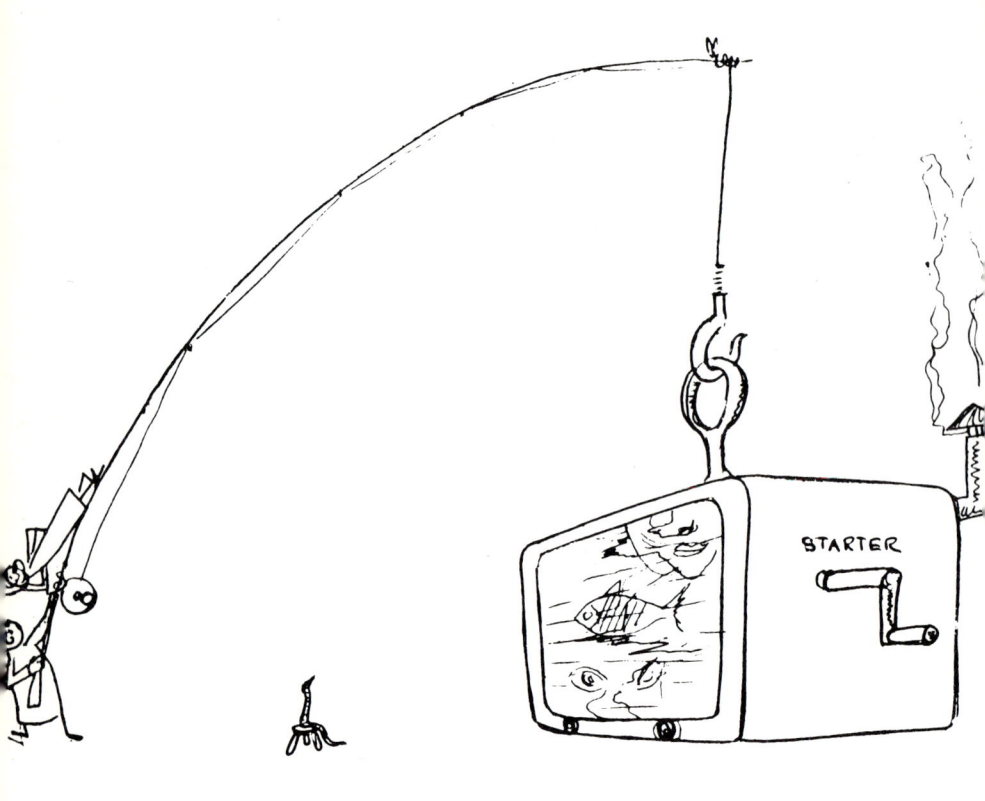

TO-DAY I SAW A LITTLE WORM

To-day I saw a little worm
Wriggling on his belly.
Perhaps he'd like to come inside
And see what's on the Telly.

TEETH

English Teeth, English Teeth!
Shining in the sun
A part of British heritage
Aye, each and every one.

English Teeth, Happy Teeth!
Always having fun
Clamping down on bits of fish
And sausages half done.

English Teeth! HEROES' Teeth!
Hear them click! and clack!
Let's sing a song of praise to them—
Three Cheers for the Brown Grey and Black.

LOOK AT ALL THOSE MONKEYS

Look at all those monkeys
Jumping in their cage.
Why don't they all go out to work
And earn a decent wage?

> *How can you say such silly things,*
> *And you a son of mine?*
> *Imagine monkeys travelling on*
> *The Morden-Edgware line!*

But what about the Pekinese!
They have an allocation.
'Don't travel during Peke hour',
It says on every station.

> *My Gosh, you're right, my clever boy,*
> *I never thought of that!*
> And so they left the monkey house,
> While an elephant raised his hat.

CAN A PARROT

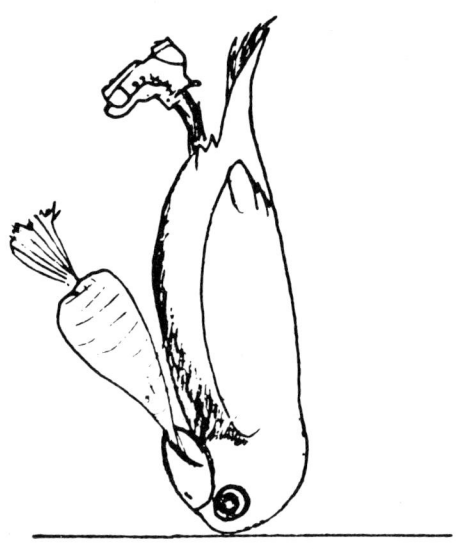

Can a parrot
Eat a carrot
Standing on his head?
If I did that my mum would send me
Straight upstairs to bed.

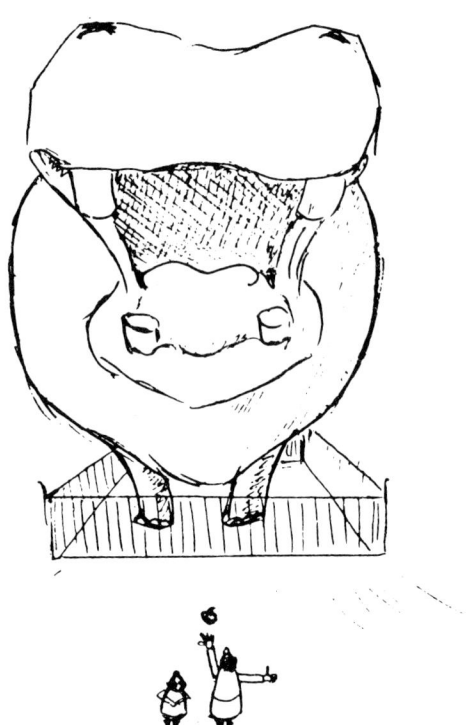

I'M NOT FRIGHTENED OF PUSSY CATS

I'm not frightened of Pussy Cats,
They only eat up mice and rats,
But a Hippopotamus
Could eat the Lotofus!

DOWN THE STREAM THE SWANS ALL GLIDE

Down the stream the swans all glide;
It's quite the cheapest way to ride.
Their legs get wet,
Their tummies wetter:
I think after all
The bus is better.

ON THE NING NANG NONG

On the Ning Nang Nong
Where the Cows go Bong!
And the Monkeys all say Boo!
There's a Nong Nang Ning
Where the trees go Ping!
And the tea pots Jibber Jabber Joo.
On the Nong Ning Nang
All the mice go Clang!
And you just can't catch 'em when they do!
So it's Ning Nang Nong!
Cows go Bong!
Nong Nang Ning!
Trees go Ping!
Nong Ning Nang!
The mice go Clang!
What a noisy place to belong,
Is the Ning Nang Ning Nang Nong!!

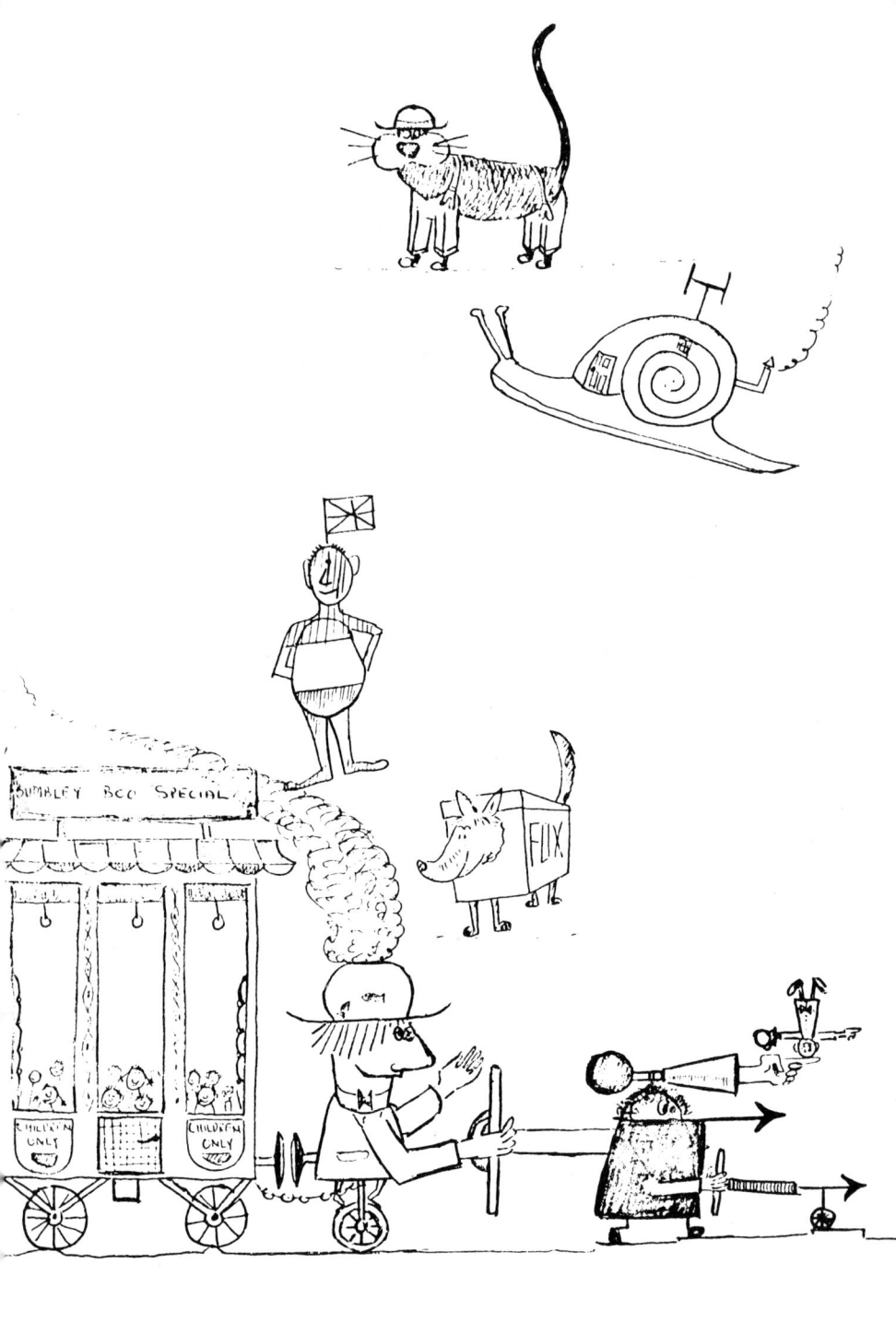

THE LAND OF THE BUMBLEY BOO

In the land of the Bumbley Boo
The people are red white and blue,
They never blow noses,
Or ever wear closes,
What a sensible thing to do!

In the Land of the Bumbley Boo
You can buy Lemon pie at the Zoo;
They give away Foxes
In little Pink Boxes
And Bottles of Dandylion Stew.

In the Land of the Bumbley Boo
You never see a Gnu,
But thousands of cats
Wearing trousers and hats
Made of Pumpkins and Pelican Glue!

CHORUS: Oh, the Bumbley Boo! the Bumbley Boo!
That's the place for me and you!
So hurry! Let's run!
The train leaves at one!
For the Land of the Bumbley Boo!
The wonderful Bumbley Boo-Boo-Boo!
The Wonderful Bumbley BOO!!!

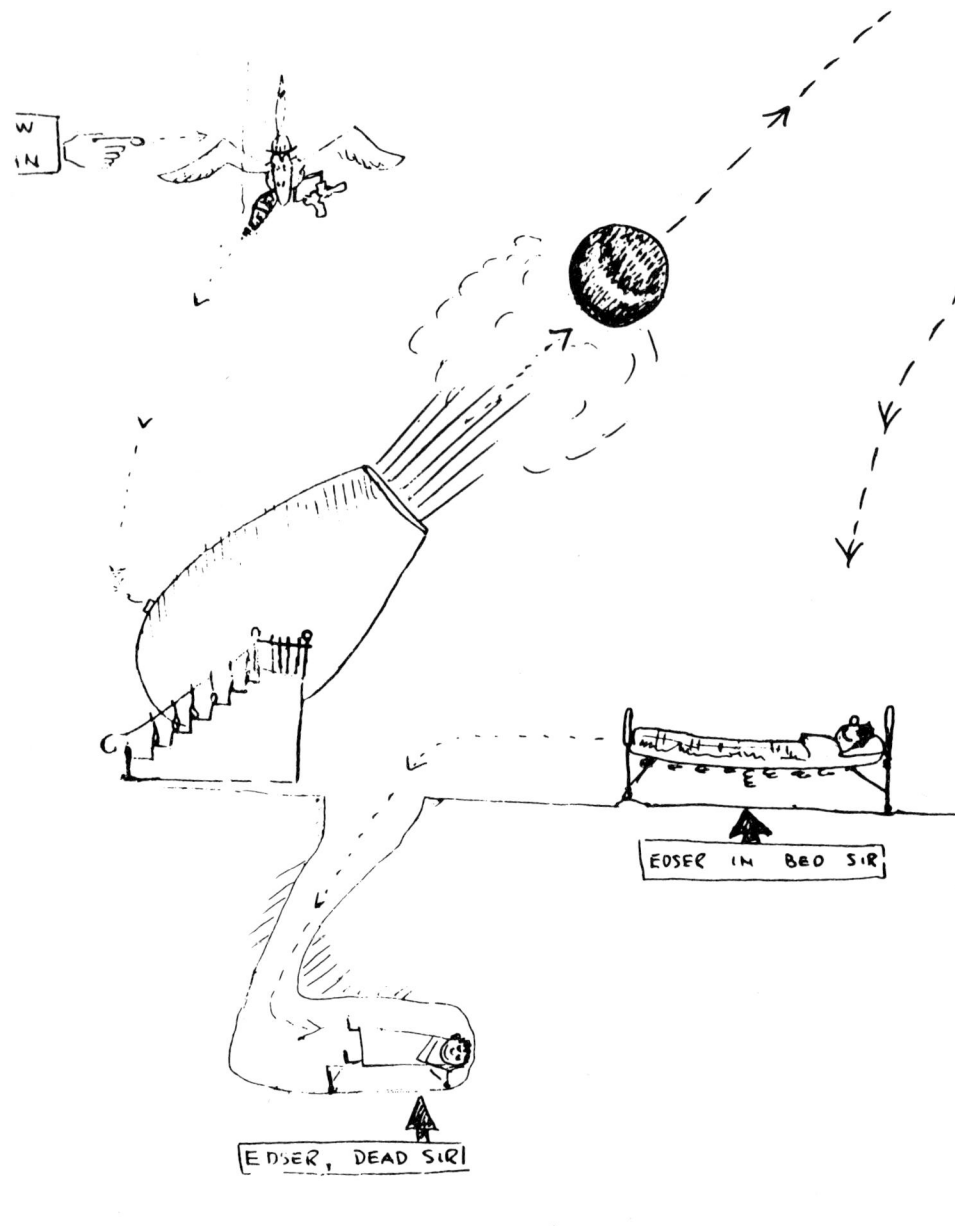

THERE WAS A YOUNG SOLDIER CALLED EDSER

There was a young soldier called Edser
When wanted was always in bed sir:
One morning at one
They fired the gun
And Edser, in bed sir, was dead sir.

YOU MUST NEVER BATH IN AN IRISH STEW

You must never bath in an Irish Stew
It's a most illogical thing to do
    But should you persist against my reasoning
    Don't fail to add the appropriate seasoning.

HELLO MR. PYTHON

Hello Mr. Python
Curling round a tree,
Bet you'd like to make yourself
A dinner out of me.

Can't you change your habits
Crushing people's bones?
I wouldn't like a dinner
That emitted fearful groans.

A THOUSAND HAIRY SAVAGES

A thousand hairy savages
Sitting down to lunch
Gobble gobble glup glup
Munch munch munch.

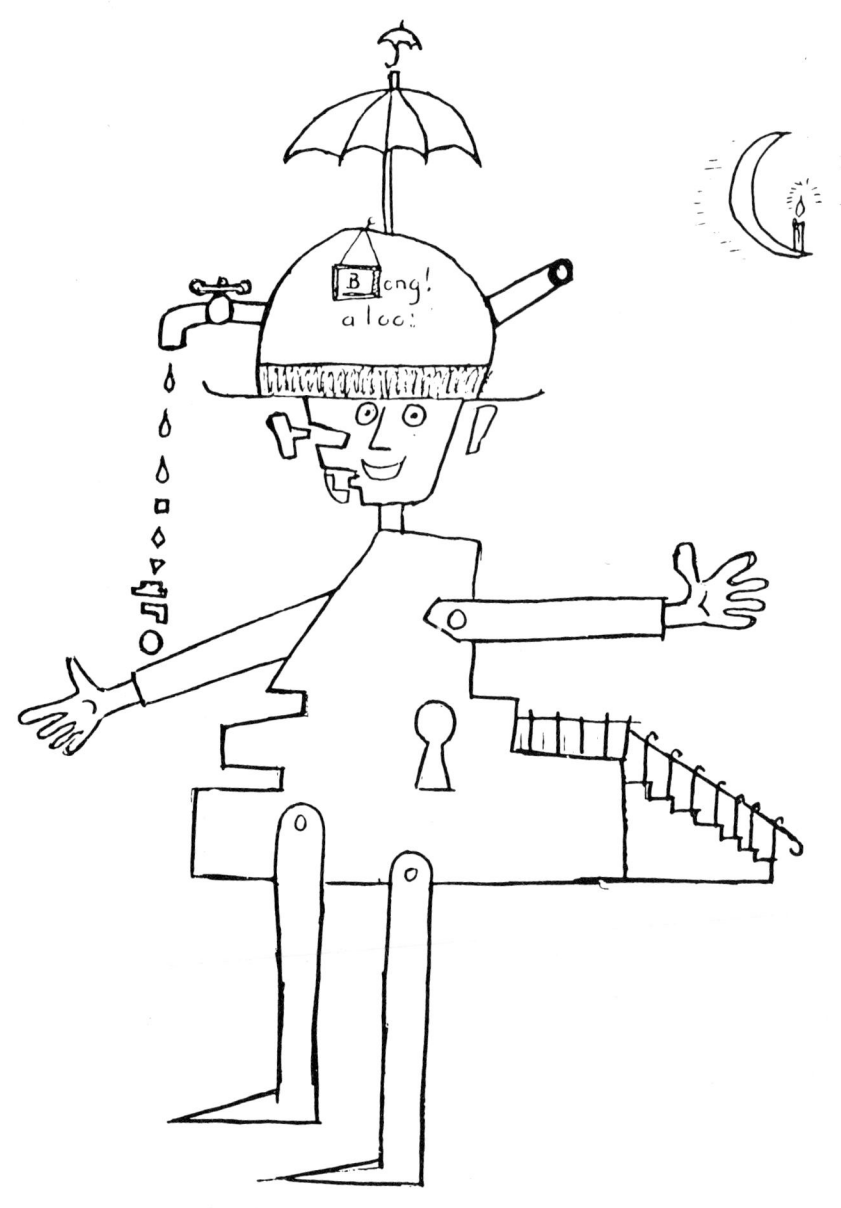

THE BONGALOO

'What is a Bongaloo, Daddy?'
'A Bongaloo, Son,' said I,
'Is a tall bag of cheese
Plus a Chinaman's knees
And the leg of a nanny goat's eye.'

'How strange is a Bongaloo, Daddy?'
'As strange as strange,' I replied.
'When the sun's in the West
It appears in a vest
Sailing out with the noonday tide.'

'What shape is a Bongaloo, Daddy?'
'The shape, my Son, I'll explain:
It's tall round the nose
Which continually grows
In the general direction of Spain.'

'Are you *sure* there's a Bongaloo, Daddy?'
'Am I sure, my Son?' said I.
'Why, I've seen it, not quite
On a dark sunny night
Do you think that I'd tell you a lie?'

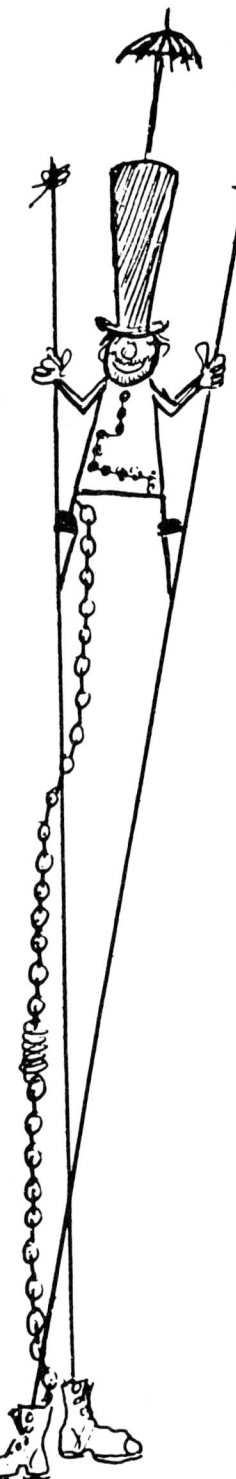

MY SISTER LAURA

My sister Laura's bigger than me
And lifts me up quite easily.
I can't lift her, I've tried and tried;
She must have something heavy inside.

FAILURE

I'm trying to write the longest first line that poetry has ever had,
For a start that wasn't bad,
Now here comes a longer oneeeeeeeeeeeeeeeeeeeeeeeeeeeeeeeeeeeeee
I know I cheated:
It was the only way I could avoid being defeated.

I ONCE KNEW A BURMESE HORSE

I once knew a Burmese horse:
Of course
He didn't know he was a horse;
But I knew Jim
So I told him—
Now he knows
And so, I close.

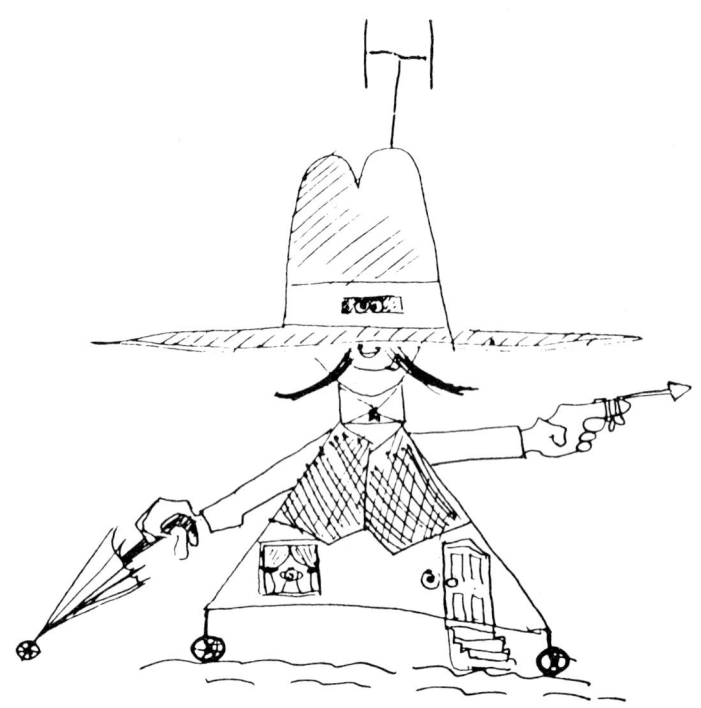

MY DADDY WEARS A BIG BLACK HAT

My daddy wears a big black hat;
He wears it in the street
And raises it to lady folk
That he perchance should meet.
He wears it on a Sunday
And on a Monday too.
He never wears it in the house,
But only out of doors.

MAVERIC

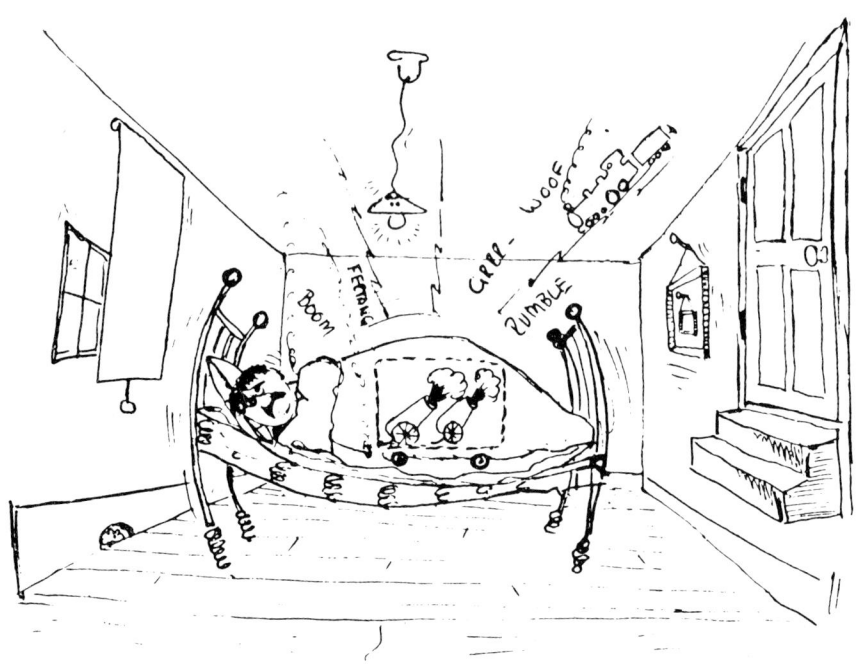

Maveric Prowles
Had Rumbling Bowles
That thundered in the night.
It shook the bedrooms all around
And gave the folks a fright.

The doctor called;
He was appalled
When through his stethoscope
He heard the sound of a baying hound,
And the acrid smell of smoke.

Was there a cure?
'The higher the fewer,'
The learned doctor said,
Then turned poor Maveric inside out
And stood him on his head.

'Just as I thought
You've been and caught
An Asiatic flu—
You mustn't go near dogs I fear
Unless they come near you.'

Poor Maveric cried.
He went cross-eyed,
His legs went green and blue.
The doctor hit him with a club
And charged him one and two.

And so my friend
This is the end,
A warning to the few:
Stay clear of doctors to the end
Or they'll get rid of you.

ON THE BRIGHT AZURIAN SEA

I have splonsoned the Splee,
And I've splansoned the Sploo,
On the Bright Azurian Sea.
I have strimbled the stroll
And the Zillikon roll,
What a wonderful place to be.
I have seen the cloor sky
O'er Klung-Lympton Rye
On the Bright Azurian Sea,
Where the Jelly-Bish stond
In the pim of your hond,
What a wonderful place to be, be,
What a wonderful place to be.

...AND ANIMALS

Part One

ANIMALS

THREE-LEGGED HIPPO

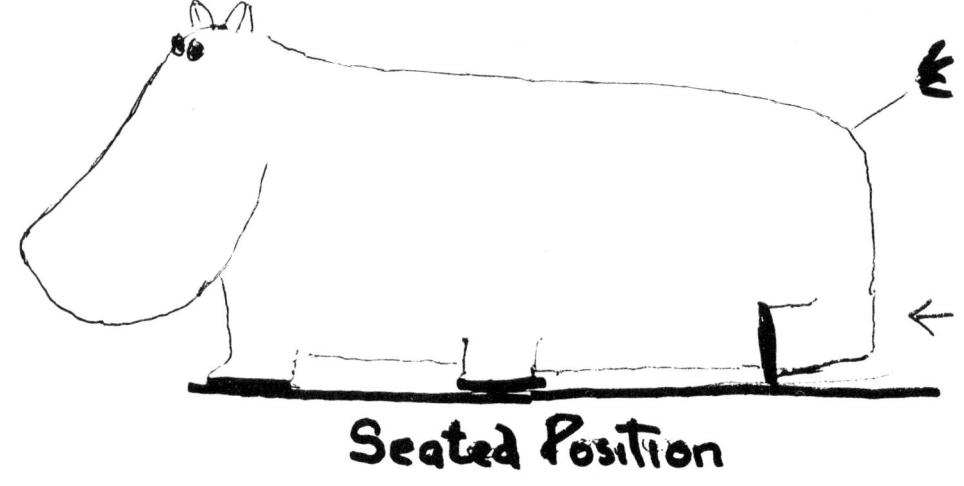

Seated Position

ARCTIC ELEPHANT

Arctic elephants are the same as African ones only they're colder. Feel one.

MOOS

Highly trained Moo-Cows doing impressions* of Moo-Zebras.

*First impression 1968

STRAWBERRY MOOSE

LEOPARDS

Leopards are easily spotted.
Just fill in the white circles with black ink.

THE CHEETAH

A sleek cat is the Cheetah,
No other could look neetah,
He's heavily dotted . . .
So he's easily spotted . . .
And he lives in Tanganyika.

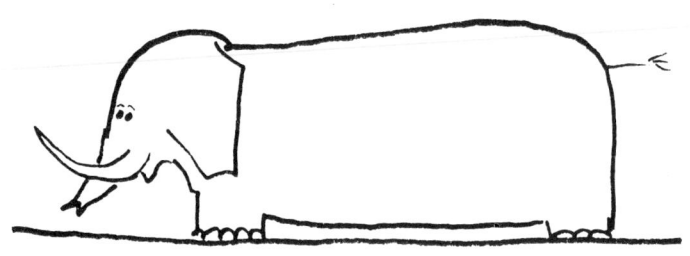

PYGMY ELEPHANT

The Pygmy Elephant is made
Much shorter that the giant brigade.
He lives much closer to the ground
And that is where he's usually found.
Why should an Elephant be so wee?
My friend, it's no good asking *me!*

ALLIGATOR

From Sydney Zoo
An Alligator
Was put on board
A flying freighter.
He ate the pilot
And the navigator
Then asked for more,
With mashed potater.

Much later

TIGER, TIGER BURNING ETC.

Tigers travel stealthily
Using, first, legs one and three.
They alternate with two and four;
And, after that, there are no more.

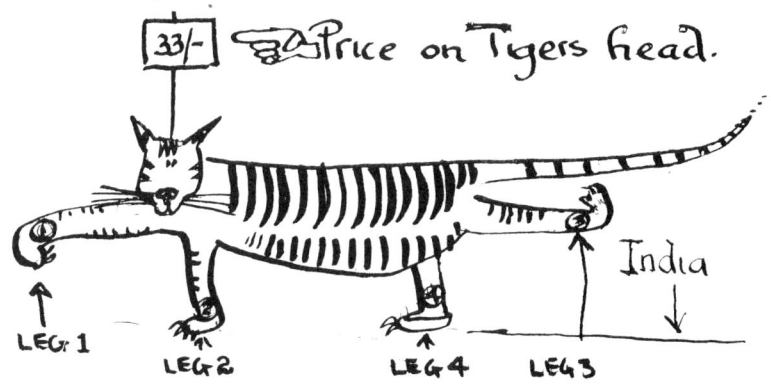

Envoi
Tiger, Tiger burning bright,
Look out! You'll set the jungle alight.

ANT AND ELEPH-ANT

Said a tiny Ant
To the Elephant,
"Mind how you tread in this clearing!"

But alas! Cruel fate!
She was crushed by the weight
Of an Elephant, hard of hearing.

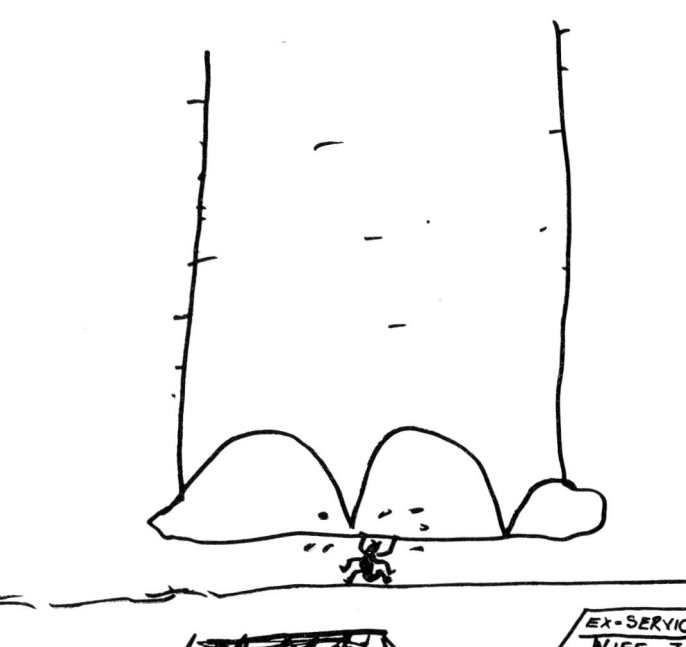

SILLY OLD BABOON

There was a Baboon
Who, one afternoon,
Said, "I think I will fly to the sun."
So, with two great palms
Strapped to his arms,
He started his take-off run.

Mile after mile
He galloped in style
But never once left the ground.
"You're running too slow,"
Said a passing crow,
"Try reaching the speed of sound."

So he put on a spurt—
By God how it hurt!
The soles of his feet caught fire.
There were great clouds of steam
As he raced through a stream
But he still didn't get any higher.

Racing on through the night,
Both his knees caught alight
And smoke billowed out from his rear.
Quick to his aid
Came a fire brigade
Who chased him for over a year.

Many moons passed by.
Did Baboon ever fly?
Did he ever get to the sun?
I've just heard today
That he's well on his way!
He'll be passing through Acton at one.

P.S. Well, what do you expect from a Baboon?

GIRAFFE No 1

We come now to
   the stately Giraffe
Who's never been known
   to smile or laugh.

But once, long ago,
   he laughed at a Tory
Who told him, they say,
   a very tall story!

GIRAFFE No 2

This self-made Giraffe
Was mentioned in despatches
For making himself
With sawdust, string and patches.

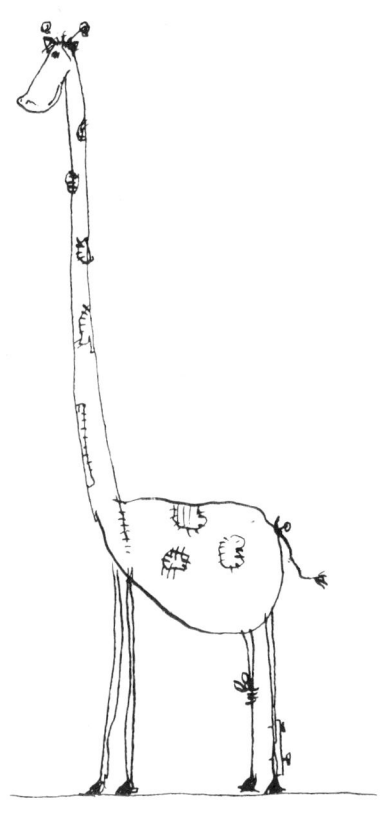

THE LION

A Lion is fierce:
His teeth can pierce
The skin of a postman's knee.

It serves him right
That, because of his bite,
He gets no letters you see.

THE PIG

A very rash young lady pig
(They say she was a smasher)
  Suddenly ran
  Under a van—
Now she's a gammon rasher.

Part Two

MILLIGANIMALS

A tourist who went to Tunisia
Said, "Are we allowed to go fishing 'ere?"
   "Oh no," said the Bey.
   "All the fish gone away.
I've only got chips on my dish in 'ere."

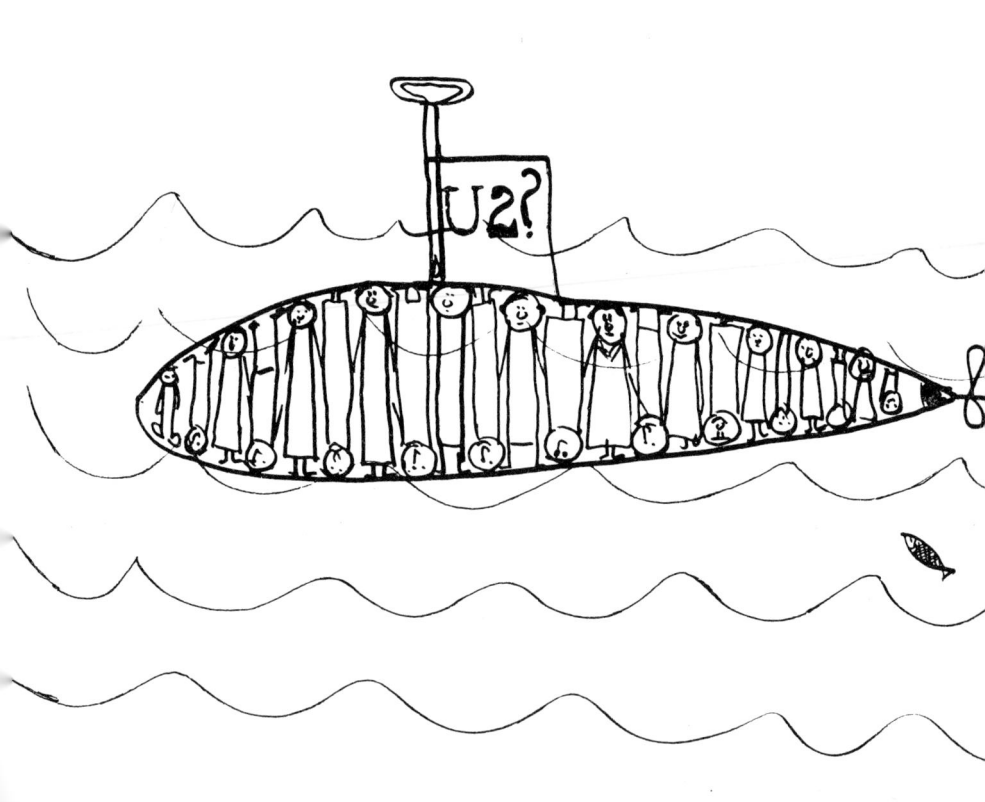

A baby Sardine
Saw her first submarine:
She was scared and watched through a peephole.

"Oh, come, come, come,"
Said the Sardine's mum,
"It's only a tin full of people."

THE ADMIRAL BYRD

You must have heard
Of the Admiral Byrd
Who found a pole called South.

He flew *all* the way
From the USA!
Well Lawdy hush ma mouth!

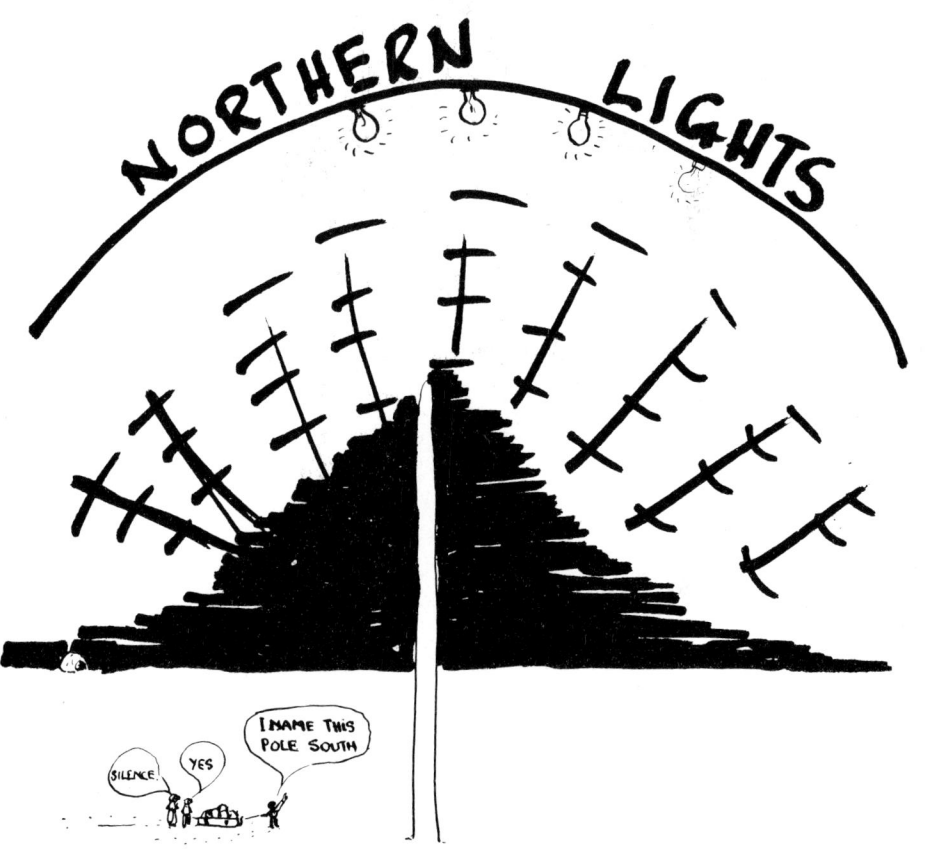

ONECAN

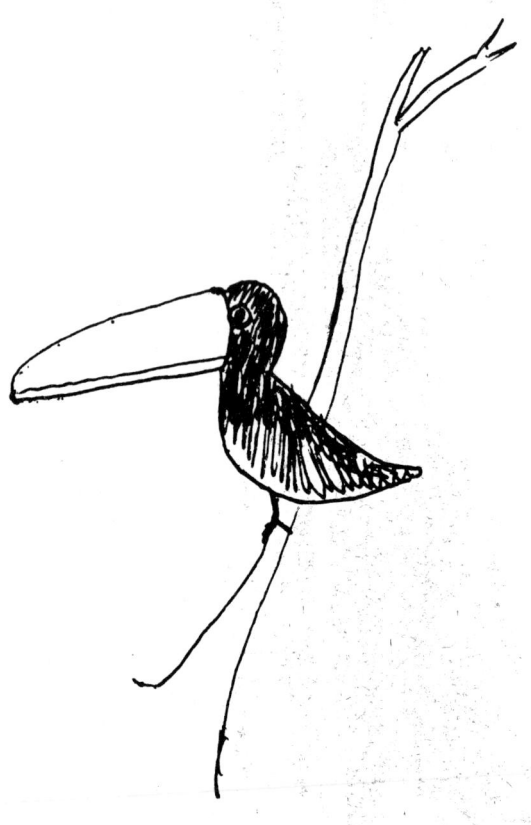

TOUCANS

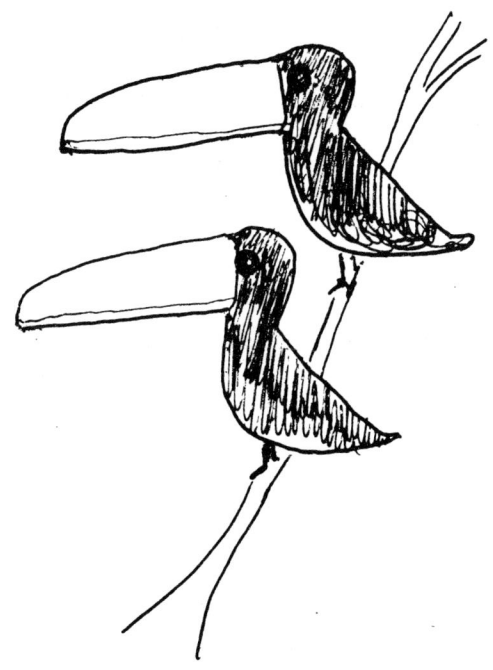

THE FLEA

How teeny teeny wee
Is the little tiny flea.
One would think that one so small
Could do no harm at all.
But all last night
In my hotel
He made me scratch
Like merry hell.

WORDS SAID

"Bunga-louie lee!"
Said the monkey to the flea.
It wasn't much to say *but*—
It passed the time away.

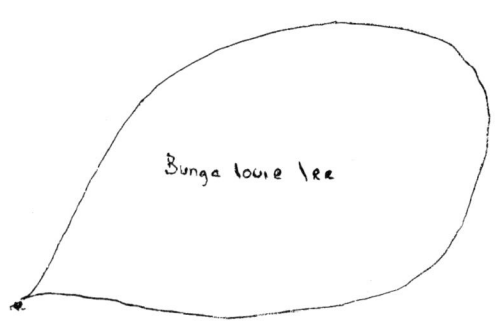

"Bunga-louie lee." Word invented by Sile when popping a hand puppet around my bedroom door. She was about seven at the time.

THE GOFONGO

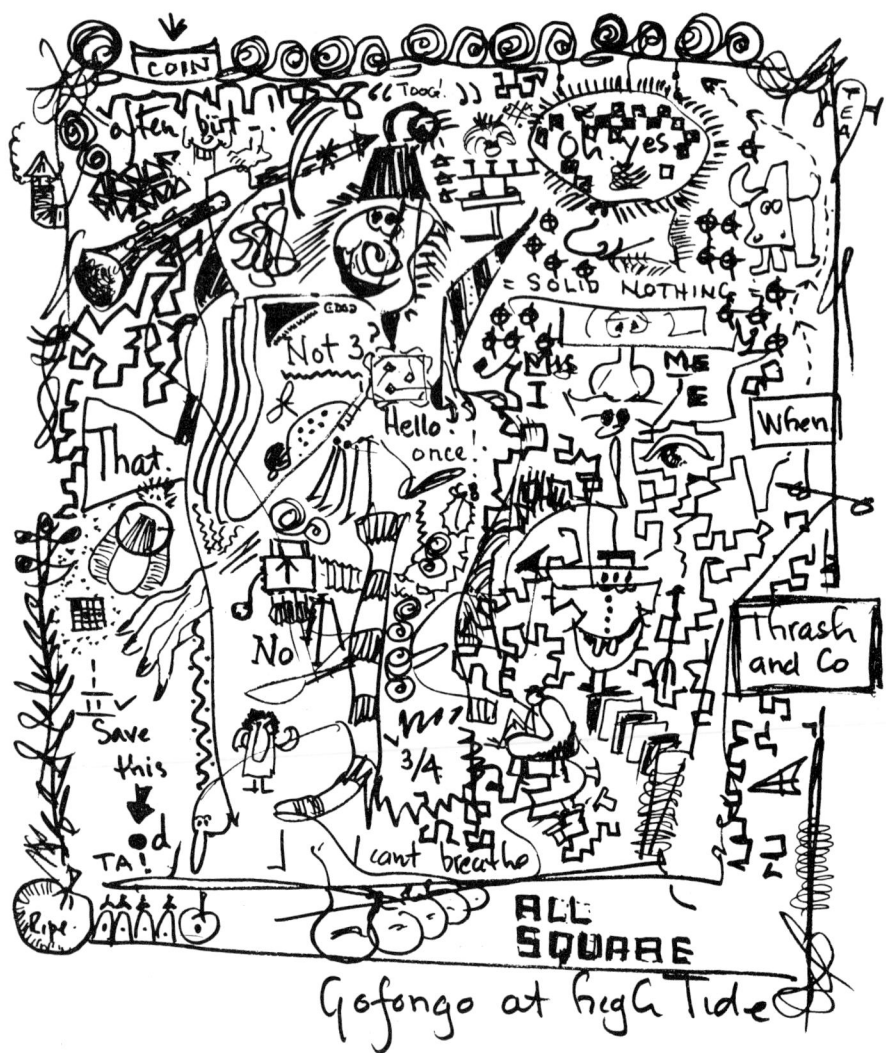

Gofongo at high Tide

The Gofongo, if you please,
Is a fish with singing knees
And a tail that plays
The Spanish clarionet!

He has toes that whistle tunes
And explode! Like toy balloons.
Hence his many,
Many visits to the vet.

The Gofongo, when he likes,
Swallows jam and rusty bikes,
Orange pips and treacle
Pudding boiled in glue.

He loves chips with rusty nails
And can swallow *iron rails*
That is why they cannot
Keep one in a zoo.

But! Gofongo as a pet
Would cause panic and regret.
People tried it and were
Nearly driven balmy.

For, once inside a house,
He screams, "I'm a Jewish mouse."
Then he runs away—
And joins the Arab Army!

WIGGLE-WOGGLE

The Wiggle-Woggle said,
"When I'm standing on my head
I can see the coast of China
And it's very, very Red."

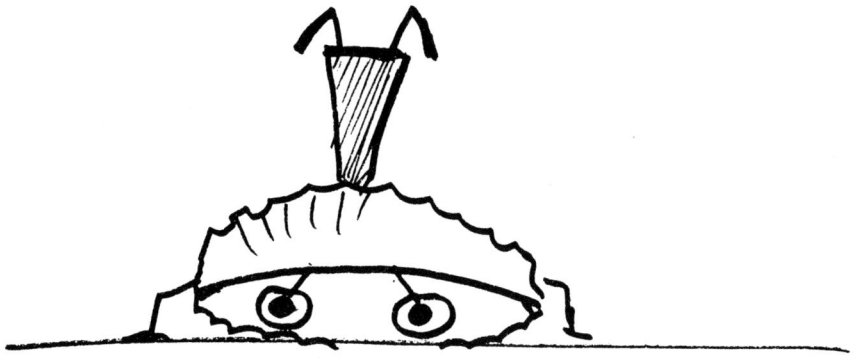

WHAT THE WIGGLE-WOGGLE SAID

The Wiggle-Woggle said,
"I wish that I were dead:
I've a pain in my tummy and
It's travelling up the bed.
I wish that I were something
That never got a pain;
A little bit of fluffy stuff
That vanished down the drain.
I could be a tiger's whisker,
A tuba made of bread,
The purple eye
Of a custard pie
With a trouser made of lead.
There *must* be other somethings—
A tiny leather bead?
Or a bit of crumpled paper
Where the water-melons feed?
A yellow thing with lumps on!
A yellow thing without!!
Some hairy stuff
On a powder puff
That snuffs the candles out.
Wish I were a lamp post

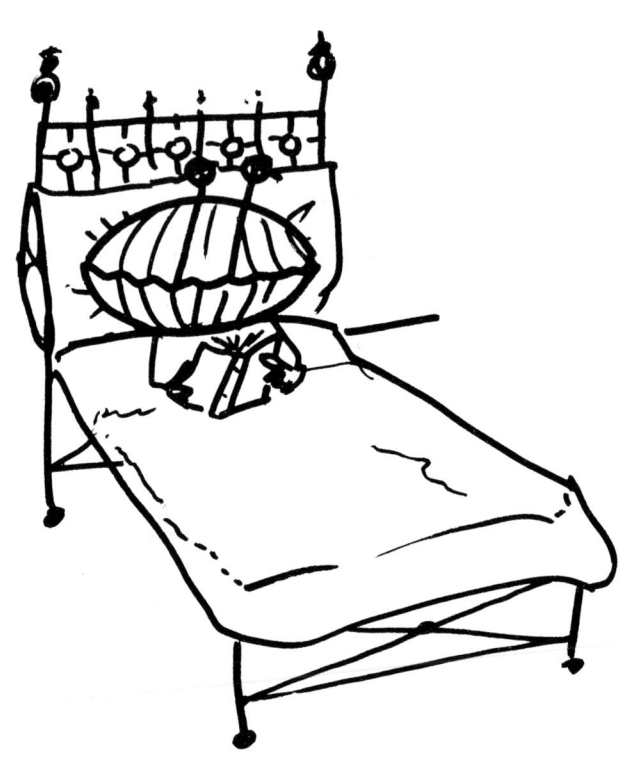

(Lamp posts don't get pains),
A leaky rusty gutter
Flooding other people's drains!
All *those* are what I'd like to be,
The Wiggle-Woggle said.

But he stayed a Wiggle-Woggle
And, what's more, he stayed in bed!

Part Three

The sad happy ending story of
THE BALD TWIT LION
A story for very all ages

Once, twice and thrice upon a time there lived a Jungle. It started at the bottom and went upwards till it reached the monkeys, who had been waiting years for the trees to reach them, and as soon as they did the monkeys invented climbing down. Most trees were made of wood, and so were the rest. Trees never spoke, not even to each other, so they never said much (actually one tree did once say "much" but nobody believed him), they never said "fish" either, not even on Fridays. It was a really good Jungle: great scarlet lilies, yellow irises, thousands of grasses all grew very happily, and this Jungle was always on time. Some people are always late, like the late King George V. But not this Jungle.

  This Jungle became very, very popular with lots of wonderful animals; there was absolutely no shortage of them and therefore the Jungle was ever so busy. This Jungle was called the Bozzollika-Dowser Jungle. Because. There was no organisation there, but *everything* worked out perfectly. Some scientists tried to make an organised Jungle of plastic, but it didn't improve conditions and the scientists left saying, "Let's go to the moon instead," and as there is nothing on the moon it seemed the best place for them. Men kept coming to the Jungle looking for gold, diamonds, gas and oil. Whereas simple animals could live without the things, brilliant man couldn't, in fact he'd forgotten how to.

One thing he never forgot was how to have wars and say, "Oh dear, how sad," when children were killed by bombs. The animals left these things called men alone. In return for this kindness man killed them, cut off their skins and put them on the floor; cut their heads off and stuck them on the walls. But if ever an animal killed a man, it was in *all* the newspapers.

But this story is a hap-hap-happy story, about animals. One day in the middle of the Jungle, near a village called Pongoland, a big lion called Mr Gronk had an attack of strongness. He was twenty-one that day and had been given the key to the Jungle, so he put on a fierce look and then, leaping in the air, he gave the biggest, loudest roar in the world. "ROAR–ROAR R☺AR!! R☺AR!!!" he went; in fact he roared so loud that it loosened all the roots of his hair and tinkle tinkle all his lovely mane fell off, and landed on the ground PLIP-PLAP-PLOP 200,000 times, one for every hair. Suddenly Mr Gronk the lion saw himself in the Daily Mirror and, oh! he saw that he was now bald! A *Bald* Lion? "Oh dearie me, I'll be the laughing stock of the hyenas," he said. So he un-roared, " ЯAoЯ! ЯAoЯ! ЯAoЯ! ," but his hairs didn't go back in, they just lay there smiling up at him, in hairy (that's hair language). Poor Mr Gronk, he now looked like a bald twit lion. As a passing hippopotamus said, "I am a passing hippopotamus,"

He roared so loud it loosened all the roots of his hairs and they fell out.

Monkey involved in Bald Twit Lion story. Also cashier at Zoo.

A Hippochondriac who was too ill to appear in the Bald Twit Lion story. So . . .

He would have looked even sillier as a one legged bald twit lion.

and went on to say, "you look like a bald hairless twit lion." When the lion heard that, he became naughty, angry and was just about to do a BIG roar, but no! he stopped, *just* in time; he'd better not roar any more, or something else might drop off him! He would look even sillier as a one-legged bald hairless twit lion, so, from then on when he was angry, he could only say very quietly, "Tsu-tsu-tsu," and there is nothing funnier than a bald hairless twit lion called Mr Gronk leaping about the Jungle going, "Tsu-tsu-tsu."

Bald Twit Lion leaping and saying, "Tsu! Tsu!"

> Part time hairy ant eater sitting on bald lions head

Part time hairy ant-eater sitting on bald lions head for the second time.

One night when he was having tea (Lyons) he said, "I can't go on being bald. It's a big problem: I must find a solution." So he squeezed every tube in the Jungle but not one had the right solution in it. Then he thought, "I'll try straining very hard and think about growing hairs." So he strained, *strained* and STRAINED, but it only made his eyes water and his nose bleed. Everyone laughed. His own flea left him. "There's nowhere to hide on a bald twit lion," he said and hopped it. He bribed a part-time hairy ant-eater to sit on his head; it really looked like real hair, but the lion got hick-ups and, each time, hairy ant-eater fell off. "I'm off," he said (which was obvious as he'd just fallen off). Lion was heart-broken. "Sad growls," he said and then did what no lion had ever done before, not even in the Ark, he laid himself down on the World and cried. "Boo-hoo, boo-hairless-hoo." The animals, having no television, gathered around him to look and feel sad. "He must have an upset tummy," said a monkey's stomach. "I would say he's had bad news," said a teenage coconut. "Rubbish," said a daft penguin and his cousin. "Lions never get bad news. No one can ever get near enough to tell them." "I think I know what it is," said an owl from his bed. "His great-great grandfather was a baboon who tried to fly to the sun, and he has just heard about it." All the animals shook their heads, and some fell off. It

Teenaged Coca-nut

Daft Penguin

Daft Penguin's
First Cousin

The crow that stood on Bald Twit Lion's nose.

wasn't a very good day for the Jungle or the animals. To make it worse a mole made a mole hill that turned into a mountain and hurt its back.

By now Bald Twit Lion had cried so much he ran out of tears, and had to drink two gallons of water, (one for each eye). Then off he went again. "Boo . . .

CHAPTER II

-hoo. Boo-hoo." All hope was not lost. A voice above him said, "Please stop crying—I've got rheumatism and all this water doesn't help." It was a lovely cross-eyed white crow (he had once been a black one, but he went colour blind making a rainbow). "Things could be worse," said Crow. "You could be a Hamlet pencil, 2B or not 2B . . ." "Oh, shut up," said Lion. "You're even making my misery miserabler." "Listen," said the Crow landing on Lion's

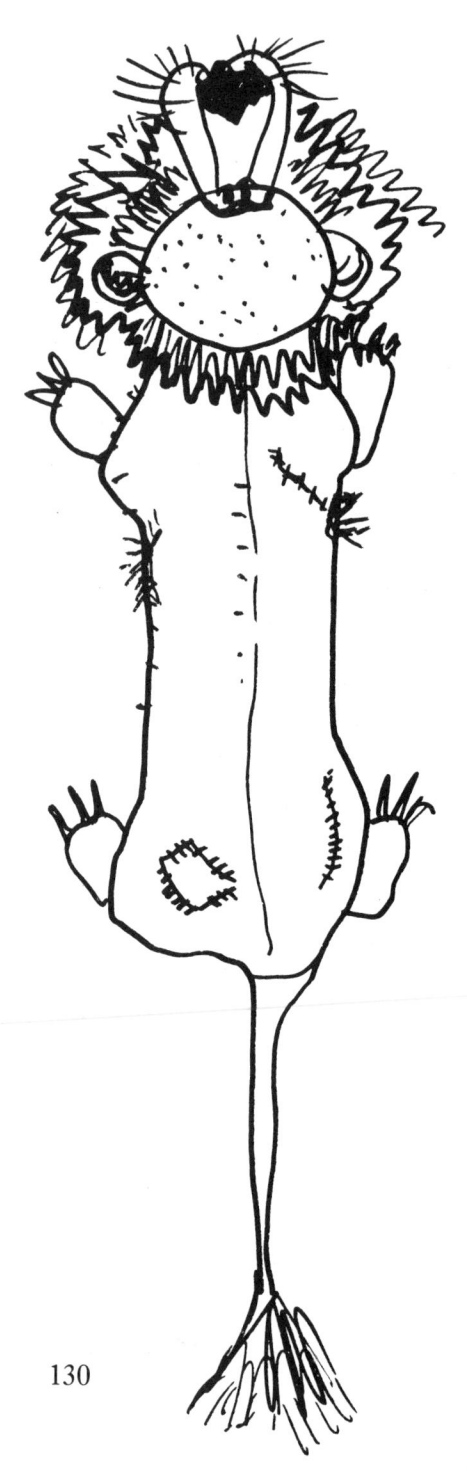

nose. "Why don't you get all the other lions to shave their heads bald then yours wouldn't notice!" Bald Twit Lion jumped to his paws "Whoopee! Saved! I've been saved. Mr White Crow, thanks," and he gave Crow a piece of knotted string as a present. Round the Jungle raced Hairless Bald Twit Lion: "Shave all your heads, or your legs will drop off!" he shouted. Soon the Jungle was alive with the sound of frightened lions shaving their heads to stop their legs falling off. In fractions it went like this:

Shave all your heads of your legs will drop off = fear

──────── = Bald Twit Lions.

shaving

Next morning the Jungle was full of hairless bald twit lions with legs and Mr Gronk was delighted.

So all that day the Jungle was a mass of leaping bald-headed lions, all looking very pleased with themselves for saving their legs. But, oh dear! Everything and every non-lion animal burst out laughing. One monkey laughed so much he fell out of his tree and krupled his blutzon, but worse still, the the lady lions were all furious with fury at their silly bald husbands, so they refused to talk or growl to

Monkey's view of Bald Twit Lion.

Daniel, snipping hairs of gorilla's chest to make lion wigs.

them. All the bald lions realised they had been spoofed. But then, along came a holy man called Daniel. He took pity on them. "Listen," he said. "I was once locked in a den of lions, and none of them bit me, and the audience asked for their money back, so it's my turn to do *you* all a good turn. So he did twenty good turns and became giddy. Then he sat down, and started to invent lions' wigs. He did it like this. After dark, Daniel would creep up to sleeping gorillas and snip-snip all the hairs off their chests. Daniel then stuck the hairs on a piece of rag, and glued them to the lion's head with nails, all except— Guess Who? Yes, poor old Mr Gronk the hairless bald twit lion. Because he was responsible for all the baldness, he was left out.

He became so sad he cried for forty days and forty nights and suffered from lakes on the knees. To make it worse there were ducks on the lake, they made such a noise at night he couldn't get to sleep so he got to wake. The quacking drove his knees deaf, in fact even if you hit stones at them they could not hear—they were stone deaf—and poor Mr Gronk had to tie ear trumpets to his legs so his knees could hear stones coming. What a picture of twit misery.

Now, you can't stop a story and leave Mr Gronk like that! No! He was still bald and it was this that changed his life. One day a party of tourists surprised Bald Twit, who was sleeping under a porridge tree

Poor Bald Twit Lion with deaf knees

for breakfast. The tourists couldn't believe their eyes, some couldn't even believe their teeth.

A bald lion? This must be the rarest animal in the world! Never in the history of the world had there ever been such a hanimule. It did not take long before great safaris of tourists were crowding the Jungle with cameras and flashlights. Mr Gronk's head became the most photographed bald head in the world, some people even took tape recordings of his baldness. His head got into the Top Ten Baldies; he out-balded Yul Brynner and Bing Crosby. Record companies even made long playing records of his bald head.

For a time he was very happy but—whereas everyone was mad to see his bald head, no one ever came to see *him*. This was the bitter end. But God was watching, he liked lions, so God slid down from Heaven on a religious giraffe's neck to the ground. "Who are you, sir," said Lion. "I am Mr God. If you don't believe me, ask Giraffe!"

Lion did, and Giraffe said, "Oh yes, he's God."

"There," said God. "If you still don't believe me, ask me a difficult question."

"O.K." said Lion. "How much is 2×2?"

"Four," said God.

"Oh yes," said Lion. "You're God all right."

"Good," said God. "Close your eyes and say 'Miggle Moggle Cake'."

Lion did. When he opened his eyes God had gone back home. But Lion now had a lovely lovely mane of beautiful black hair, and he was so happy he married a Roman Catholic giraffe and lived happily ever after until the next day.

End of Kid's book.
Start here for Grown-ups!

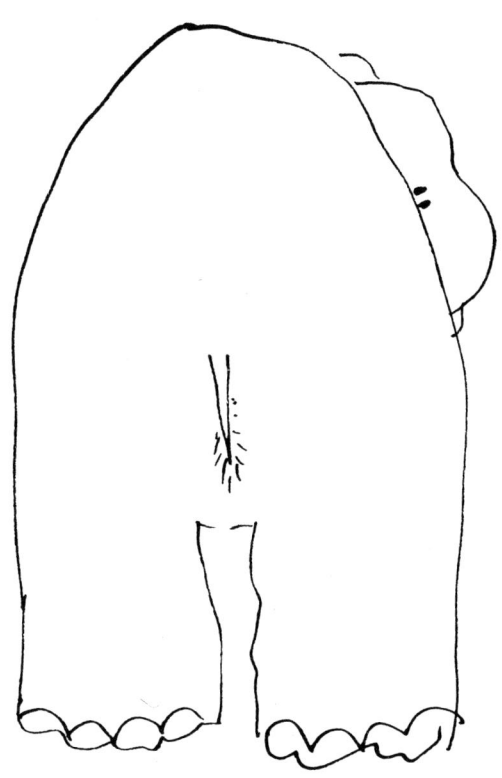

THE END

SG2